D1082651

Brokenhearted
Parents

Brokenhearted
Parents

*A Workbook for Parents Hurting
over Adult Children*

Sharon Grinder

RESOURCE *Publications* · Eugene, Oregon

BROKENHEARTED PARENTS
A Workbook for Parents Hurting over Adult Children

Resource Publications
An Imprint of Wipf and Stock Publishers
199 W. 8th Ave., Suite 3
Eugene, OR 97401

www.wipfandstock.com

ISBN 13: 978-1-4982-0152-0

Manufactured in the U.S.A.

Dedicated to my parents, Merle and Helen Chansler (my mom is now in heaven) who have loved me unconditionally all my life and have prayed for me daily. I thank God for them and for the wonderful privilege of being raised in a Christ-centered home. That foundation of Christ has helped me in many hard and difficult storms in my life.

"In the same way, the Spirit helps us in our weakness. We do not know what we ought to pray for, but the Spirit himself intercedes for us with groans that words cannot express. And he who searches our hearts knows the mind of the Spirit, because the Spirit intercedes for the saints in accordance with God's will."

—ROM 8:26

Contents

Preface

THIS BOOK IS FROM my heart to yours. I pray that you will find this as helpful to you as it was helpful for me to write it. I have experienced a fractured relationship with my older daughter and I am in the midst of the healing process. It has been helpful to learn to let God be God and realize that he is in control—not me. My express purpose in writing this is to help others as I have been helped. It is too easy to get stuck in grief and not move forward. God can carry you through your pain and trials and make you stronger, more compassionate and a lot deeper of a person in Christ. God will also give you opportunities to minister to others with more caring and understanding than if you had never gone through this time in your life.

Take out of this book what reaches to your heart and needs. We all need to work through things in our own personal way. As a pastor's wife for thirty-four years and a churchgoer for more years than that, I have had many parents come and share with me how brokenhearted they are over the ways their adult children have gone. The pain can be overwhelming at times, but be assured that God knows all about it—he knows your heart, your prayers, and your love for your child. He also knows his ways and those ways not necessarily ours. His will may be worked out through a long process of time or may come quickly. May working through this book be a time of soul searching, growing, and learning what God wants to do in your life. The love that God has for you and your child goes beyond what you can see or comprehend. May you be able to embrace this time of your life as a chance to grow a deeper, closer, and more surrendered relationship to the Lord. God bless you in this particular journey of your life.

Sharon Grinder

Acknowledgments

I WANT TO THANK SOME very special people for contributing, helping, praying, and encouraging me with this book: Kathi Quiring, Leesa Henselman, Denette Fretz and Janet Hawkins. You are very special to me. Thank you all!

Introduction

THIS BOOK CAN BE used to help you process your feelings as you deal with the relationship issues with your adult child. There are chapters to read, questions to answer, and spaces to journal. Additionally, there are song suggestions at the end of each chapter to help you deepen your personal time.

As an artist, I have been able to express my thoughts and prayers more fully when I draw them. You will have opportunities to draw out your thoughts and prayers in this journal. Don't worry—it's not an art contest, just another way to express your feelings. You can develop ways to express yourself in devotionals, prayer, music, etc. Seeking your relationship with the Lord and his wisdom is the main goal and purpose of this book. May you find God's peace in your personal storm.

Guidelines for this Workbook

1. If at any time you feel you are suffering more than you can handle please get help from a doctor or counselor. You don't need to suffer alone and without professional help.

2. Pray and seek God's guidance before you even say a word to your child.

3. Treat your child with love and respect even if you feel like they don't deserve it.

4. Speak respectfully of your child to others. Tearing your child down because you're hurt or are in pain does not help in the healing process, can cause your child to not trust you, and deepen the distance between you.

5. Do your best to be a living example of the love of Christ by taking on the attitude of Christ (Phil 2:5–8).

6. Take time to answer the questions, journal, pray, and draw your hopes, dreams, and prayerful desires for your child, as you work through this book.

I

What is a Broken Heart?

A BROKEN HEART IS A hurt that pierces your very soul; a pain that burns deep; a feeling like there's a heavy weight on your chest and you can't take a deep breath. When my older daughter first told my husband and me that she was pulling away from us, it was the worst feeling of rejection I had ever known. I lost weight and went into a season of grief and loss. I had to process and work through my feelings, and search for the direction God wanted me to go and to learn what he needed me to learn.

The psalms talk a lot about the brokenhearted. Psalm 34:18 says, "The Lord is close to the brokenhearted and saves those who are crushed in Spirit." Being brokenhearted is not a sin. In fact, God is especially close to us when we are brokenhearted. However, being brokenhearted is not a blanket to cower under either. Experience it. Grow in it. Love through it. Cry about it. Pray over it. Don't drown or wallow in it. Don't allow it to eat you up and pull you down to a place where it's hard to be picked up again. Work your way through it with prayer and determination and find God pulling you up and giving you strength.

A broken heart can come in many forms:

- a child who makes choices that are not healthy, emotionally or spiritually right
- a child who comes in conflict with another parent, spouse, or siblings
- a child who is a chronic liar and deceiver
- a child who seems to be easily swayed by friends, relatives, and others
- a child lost in addictions
- a child who lets their own pride be their guide and will not be submissive to God's precepts.

The list could go on and on. We each have our own stories to tell and our own pain to work through.

The initial responses to a fractured relationship with an adult child can be varied:

- fight or angrily confront them
- run away from the pain in various venues
- feel cornered or trapped, or harbor pent up inward anger
- extreme "rollercoaster" emotions
- continuous crying
- loss of appetite or too much appetite (stress-eating)
- feel physically sick to your stomach
- experience a loss of breath
- feel the impulse to fix it ("Band-Aid it up")
- correct misinterpretations that you think they have or make your exact feelings known so nothing is taken out of your context
- the desire to "shake some sense" into the person.

The person you are brokenhearted over may not even accept any responsibility for your pain. They feel it's your own fault that you are miserable and deny any part of your grief. They could even point out your feelings as a weakness. Know what you know. Stand firm in Jesus. Love them no matter what and use this opportunity to draw closer to God than you ever have in your life. If you let anger resentment, frustration, bitterness, or grief take control, you will eventually realize that you are being controlled by emotions rather than letting God be in control of you and the situation. Another obstacle that can come up is the idea that if you don't believe the way they want you to, they will reject you, even though you tell them you love them no matter what they are doing. When the choice comes down to believing in and following God's word or rejecting your beliefs for your relationship, what are you going to choose?

Questions to Help You Process:

Do I feel brokenhearted?

What are my responses to my situation?
(Look at the list above for some examples)

Can I pinpoint the real causes of my broken heart?

What are some ways I can work on each item and what are some items I can't fix?

Do I want to work through these items?

How can I work through them inside myself?

What does God want me to do?

What are my choices?

Where can God take my spiritual life through this journey?

Song: *"Does Jesus Care?" by Frank Graeff & Lincoln Hall*

Journal or draw your thoughts from this lesson:

2

Trying to Understand Rebelliousness

TRYING TO UNDERSTAND THE incomprehensible—a rebellious spirit—isn't easy. Rebelliousness doesn't necessarily make sense, nor is it readily fixable. Your child may not even be able to explain it to themselves much less to you. God gives our children a certain amount of independence so that they can break away into their own families eventually. However, a rebellious attitude can sometimes become extreme and disrespectful. The tendency to be unreasonable is a part of a rebellious spirit.

What can I do when I can't make sense of rebellion and my child doesn't make sense to me at all? What happened to make my child turn 180 degrees away from God, from me, from foundations that were laid in my child's life, from being soft to being hard, from being able to share to having a communication lock down? Sometimes it's the very restraints a child may feel about Christianity that makes them want to rebel and go against what they know is right. In other words, the very knowledge of what is right can compel them to want to do the opposite. There are other causes for rebellion: trying to be noticed, doing something radically different than usual, thinking that new ways are better, the influences of others around them, wanting more than they have, and dealing with boredom.

As much as you may disagree with your child's opinions because of your own view of the issues or the biblical scriptures on it, what cost do you want it to have in your relationship? Some parents choose to ignore the problem, cut off their relationship with their child, or conversely, try to keep the doors open however they can. It may take some trial and error time to figure out how to handle the situation because you may be so blown away that you don't know what to do. Try to keep the communication level flowing as much as possible through whatever venues you can: e-mail, texting, letters, phone calls, Facebook, visits, etc. Try to make your communication as non-confrontational as possible. Keep respect of their boundaries but also keep your own as well. Always, "speak the truth in love" (Eph 4:15). But if there's unwillingness to listen to what you say, find common ground where you can talk easily and make it especially important to listen to them. Listen to the Holy Spirit's prompting on what to say and when to say it (not your own humanness) at the right time and place. Some levels of communication take time to build up again to the easy fun rapport that maybe you once had. If you do have to confront an issue, be careful to not confront if you are in a vulnerable mood when you might get angry, frustrated, or cry and cause more strain in the relationship. Try all you can to keep the communication levels open and live without regrets. Also, show respect for them by not putting them down to anyone else who will listen. It may come back to haunt you and destroy anything you've tried so hard to build up.

If we knew the "why" of rebelliousness, would we try to fix it? Would we try to control it? Walking by faith is hard because we can't see ahead of us. Real faith takes us to a deeper level of trust in our Lord and Savior. God is in control—not us.

Questions to Help You Process:

Was there ever a time when I was rebellious?

What did it take for me to work through that time?

Where do I think my child's rebelliousness stems from?

Do I need to figure out their rebellious attitude to get help and healing for me?

In what ways can I communicate with my child without conflict?

If I don't have any communication with my child for whatever reason, how can I deal with it?

If it's a one-sided communication from me to them only, how can I deal with it?

Should I commit to carrying on a one-sided conversation?

What can I do to make a step towards healing my relationship with my child?

Can I avoid putting my child down to others?

If I feel I need to talk with someone else about my situation how can I relate my feelings without saying negative and hurtful things about my child?

Where can God take my spiritual life through this journey?

Song: "Blessings" by Laura Story

Journal or draw your thoughts from this lesson:

3

Can I Talk to Someone?

FIND SOMEONE YOU CAN trust, who understands the things you are dealing with, and who shares your values. Talking to someone who lacks understanding or sympathy can be like salt rubbed in an open wound. They cause more pain and confusion and don't really help with answers because they don't really understand. Some may want to give you a quick Band-Aid answer. They don't want to see, work with or experience your pain. They want it to go away so everyone can feel better and not deal with it anymore. Find someone who will listen, pray with you, and not lay heavy convictions or guilt on you: God, a spouse, friend, counselor, pastor, mentor, etc. Make prayer your focus instead of fretting. Journaling is extremely helpful, too. It lets you get all your feelings out of your head and onto paper where you can see it and learn what's in your heart in a more visual way. Then you can realistically analyze and come up with concrete ways to help you deal with your situation.

God

"Cast all your anxiety on him because he cares for you" (1 Pet 5:7). You can trust in God as a safe place to share your grief because he cares about you, right where you are, right now, and he knows what is going on, not only on the outside, but on the inside as well. Believe in the power of prayer and the help of prayer in talking with the Almighty God. Psalm 116:1 says: "I love the Lord, for he heard my voice; he heard my cry for mercy. Because he turned his ear to me, I will call on him as long as I live."

Do you have trouble spending time with God in prayer? Many have a hard time concentrating when there are so many distractions around. One helpful idea is to have a daily devotional page that you can keep on your computer and print out with all the areas of prayer you want to cover (look for a personal devotional page idea in the back of this book). When I use my devotional page, I have it in front of me when I'm reading and praying. I jot down thoughts, feelings and prayers as I go. This keeps my mind from wondering off in a dozen different directions. The beautiful thing about prayer is that when we pray, God knows all about our lives, thoughts, and feelings—we can share freely with him without any barriers. When you can't sleep, the best pastime is to pray. Prayer is not about God giving me what I want. It's about spending time with him, getting to know him better, and to learn what his will is in our lives.

Journaling

Journal about all your feelings. A journal has no opinion or judgments of you and just lets you vent. Draw your feelings, desires, hopes, and dreams as a part of your journaling. It is very helpful to see what you hope for in picture form, even if its stick figures and only you know what it is. A journal doesn't have to be an expensive blank book from an elegant bookstore. It can be a spiral notebook (they're really cheap during the back to school season), theme book, or something you can find at a dollar type of store. But a journal can be priceless to release pent up emotions and to go over later to see how far God has brought you. It can also help you to see how you really are feeling and help you look at your situation more objectively. If you'd rather others didn't look at your innermost feelings, don't leave it out for viewing. Throw away the passages you don't what to keep.

Other People

Spouses, friends, counselors, mentors, or pastors are other people to share with. Seek counsel from a godly person you can trust—someone who will respect your privacy and keep from sharing your conversation with others. Choose someone you perceive as a person sound in the faith and strong in their relationship with God. Getting a new insight can be very helpful in your journey, especially if you're stuck trying to figure things out. You can find a list of Christian counselors through a church, work of mouth, or on the internet. Even some Christian counselors may not have your views on certain issues. They may not be as compassionate about your feelings and thus not be as helpful as you would like them to be. Find a person that challenges you to grow and who is willing to help you work through the process. Healing takes time. We don't expect an open physical wound to heal immediately. Neither should we expect that an emotional wound would mend without time and proper treatment to heal.

Remember that no one person is going to make it all go away or make everything right again. That's God business. In other words, try not to put all your hopes into one human basket. God will guide you to the right direction or path he wants you to go.

Questions to Help You Process:

Do I need to make more time with God to get closer to him and talk with him more about my broken relationship with my child?

What can I do to make my time with God more meaningful?

Do I need to get a journal?

What kind of plan do I need to make to keep my journal
(e.g. schedule a time each day, use it when needed,
categories such as praise or prayer)?

Who is someone I can trust?

What are my expectations of that someone?

Am I being realistic about those expectations?

Where can God take my spiritual life through this journey?

*Songs: "I Must Tell Jesus" by Elisha Hoffman and "What a Friend
We Have in Jesus" by Joseph Scriven & Charles Converse*

Journal or draw your thoughts from this lesson:

4

A Look at the Prodigal Son

(Read Luke 15:11–24)

IN THE LUKE ACCOUNT of the prodigal son, we learn that the son left and lived a wild lifestyle, came to a point of crisis—which caused him to take a realistic look at his life—and came home to a waiting and forgiving parent. Seeing your child wallow in the mud of a sinful lifestyle is very heartbreaking. Knowing that your child is doing the very things you have tried so hard to keep out of their life and protect them from is something that can cause grief, pain, and tears.

Everyone has the freedom to choose or reject. God wants us to come to him willingly—not forced or coerced. If we come to God unwillingly, it's not out of love, respect, or desire to follow him, but grudgingly and out of resentment, which is really not a relationship of love at all. In the story of the prodigal son, the father didn't beg him to stay, but rather gave him his inheritance and let the son go. He looked for his son to come back, but let him do so on his own.

Remember in the story that when the son came to his senses, it was at a point of crisis in his life. At that time he remembered the good points about home and what he was missing. The son's main focus was to be a servant so he could eat, but his father just wanted his son returned to him. When he got back, his father didn't lecture him on how he had lived, but took him back with love and celebration. Are you willing to wait and pray and stand with open arms? Are you ready to forgive when your child comes back to God and/or you?

Jesus said in Matt 23:37, "O Jerusalem, Jerusalem, you who kill the prophets and stone those sent to you, how often I have longed to gather your children together, as a hen gathers her chicks under her wings, but you were not willing." God is familiar with the pain of the many times the Israelites rebelled away from his relationship with him. He understands our pain. He never forced the Israelites back. They had to be willing. They lived in their sin by their own will. They had to desire relationship with him; we can't make our children respond to God. They have to be willing. Ultimately, their walk with God is their own choice. Pray for them to be willing and wait for them with open arms.

Questions for you to help you process:

Am I too concerned about how I think others view me and my situation with my prodigal?

The parable of the lost sheep is in the same chapter of Luke as the prodigal son (read Luke 15:1–7). In the same chapter is the parable of the lost coin (read Luke 15:8–10). Why were these stories on seeking the lost told by Jesus?

Are the ones who wander off important to him?

Do I trust in the Lord to earnestly seek my child?

Do I love my child more than Jesus does?

Does my child have free will to choose the Lord or not like I do?

Draw a picture, write a poem or piece of prose showing your relationship being healed.

Where can God take my spiritual life through this journey?

Songs: *"Draw Me Close To You" by Michael W. Smith and*
"You're Not Alone" by Meredith Andrews

Journal or draw your thoughts from this lesson:

5

What is the Difference Between Concern, Worry, and Fretting?

I BELIEVE WE ARE SUPPOSED to be concerned. I believe we are supposed to be giving our worries and concerns to Jesus. I also believe we are not supposed to fret. And yet with our children facing very real and present dangers (some of which they do not seem to recognize as real and present) the temptation to fret is very strong. This is especially true if what they are doing is potentially life threatening. Fretting is the gut wrenching, dreadful fear of what could happen to them. Fretting is possessive, strong, and consuming. It can make you ill, bring bitterness, cause you to lose hope, and fill all your thoughts. Psalm 37:8b says "do not fret—it leads only to evil." The evil it can bring is not only to others but especially to us. It drains us emotionally and physically and pulls us away from where God wants us to be. We know we shouldn't let it take us over. Easier said than done, right? When others try to remind us of the "not being anxious" verses, it can sometimes turn our feelings to guilt, anger, and despair. We don't understand why we can't turn it off to peace and trust automatically like flipping a light switch. On occasion we would just like our friends to be understanding and not preach at us. The way we let go of worry and fretting is to study God's word, pray a lot and deepen our trust that God will do what is divinely right and just. It can be learning process that can take some time to sink in because we feel more secure and in control when we hold on to it. Can you trust God so much that, whatever happens, you know that he is ultimately in control and has his own plan?

I believe that worry is the first step towards fretting. The situation goes over and over in our minds but hasn't gotten so intense that it's our only thought. In Phil 4:6–7, the Bible says: "Do not be anxious about anything, but in everything, by prayer and petition, with thanksgiving, present your requests to God. And the peace of God, which transcends all understanding, will guard your hearts and your minds in Christ Jesus." You can find ways to help turn off the "worry syndrome" by putting your thoughts and energies into something else more worthwhile, like helping others.

Concern is caring without worrying or fretting; it is knowing the situation, caring about it, lifting it to God, and trusting him for the outcome. Concern is the ability to not concentrate on all the possible negative outcomes that could happen but to let it go and live in the present, not the unpredictable future.

A beautiful reminder to me that God cares about me and that I shouldn't fret is when Jesus calls himself the Good Shepherd. He lovingly tends his sheep, not as a hired hand, but as someone who cares. When I picture him seeking the lost as the kind and gentle shepherd, I feel calmer about my concerns.

Questions to Help You Process:

What does fret do for me?

What does fret do against me?

Why would I want to hold on to fretting?

Do I feel like not worrying or fretting means I don't care?

Can I list some ways to care without fretting?

Can I find an area of concern in myself that doesn't give way to fretting?

Can you separate the idea of being lovingly concerned about your child and worrying about them?

Have your ever experienced the "Peace that passes understanding"?
(Phil 4:7)

In Phil 4:7, what does Jesus guard your heart with?

If something is eating you up and you're heading in a self-destructive direction, is it worth it?

Look at Phil 4:8. What am I to think about?

Where does God want me to be in my thoughts?

Spend time in the first nine verses of Ps 37. Underline key words. What key words do I especially want to hold on to?

What does God want you to spend your time doing?

Can you picture you are turning channels on the radio or TV. Can you turn the channel of Fret by turning it off and turning onto the channels of Trust, Commit, Delight, etc. instead?

Can I see Jesus being the Good Shepherd and earnestly seeking my child?

Where can God take my spiritual life through this journey?

Song: *"Cares Chorus" by Kelly Willard*

Journal or draw your thoughts from this lesson:

6

Letting Go?

W E MIGHT GET TIRED of hearing about letting things go to God, but honestly we have very little control, if any. Is our situation really in our hands anyway? It's like the kiddie car ride at the fair where the children happily spin the drivers' wheel, but in reality, the track is the only thing that guides the car. God has a plan (Jer 29:11). God has his timing (Eccl 3:1). Can you let it go and know that you are not in control of whatever happens with your child's walk with God, or their relationship with you? You can pray and seek, but you are not in control. That may be hard to hear and even harder to do.

When your child was small, you could control where they went, when they did activities and homework, what they ate, and when they went to bed. You may have even taken them to the doctor kicking and screaming because you knew their health was more important that what they wanted to do. You were used to guiding them in many ways. But now, in reality you are only in control and responsible for your own walk. It's important to nurture your own walk with God. When Jesus talked with Peter after his death, Peter wanted to know the plans Jesus had for John. Jesus said "If I want him to remain alive until I return, what is that to you? You must follow me" (John 21:22). We need to work on our own relationship with God because that is the real center of our lives—*not our situation*. Our situation can color our whole world, if we let it.

Letting go is like ungrasping a rope we've held onto for a long period of time and not knowing where we are going to drop. It can be a terrifying feeling, making us think we need to do something. When a person grasps something tightly for a long period of time, their hands can become stiff and frozen to the object. When we willingly hand over the control to God and let him to what he wants, it means: ". . . not my will, but yours be done" (Luke 22:42). Letting go doesn't mean we let go of our love or deep prayers for our child. But it means trusting God to guide them where we can't, letting God influence them in places where we aren't, God speaking to their heart where they won't listen to us, letting God work in his own timing, and letting God's plan for your child come into fulfillment. Can you trust God on a deeper level that may be much more than you've ever trusted? Unfreeze your hands.

When I have come to the end of myself, I find that the things of the world are worthless to me and I come empty before God with nothing else to give, no pretense, and wearing nothing superficial. I find him loving me and satisfying me with his presence in a way that is joyful, open, and honest. In the well known and loved children's book, *The Velveteen Rabbit* by Margery Williams, the toy rabbit and the skin horse have a discussion about becoming real. The old skin horse tells the Velveteen Rabbit, "When a child loves you for a long, long time, not just to play with, but really loves you, then you become real." In another instance he says that, "once you become real you can't be ugly, except to people who don't understand." God loves you so, so much and wants to make you real. You can never be ugly to him. He sees beyond the junk and the mistakes and sees the potential and the beauty of who we are and want to be. He takes the hard times in your life and makes you a real person, a person that stands in honesty before him with no pretense. You can come to know him deeper when you have surrendered all you have and all you are before him. When we are fully surrendered to God in love and awe, he is able to do more in us and through us than we have ever before experienced. It's a beautiful thing to become real.

Questions to Help You Process:

What is my will and what is God's will?

What do I need to let go of?

Can you put your child totally into God's hands, unfreeze your hands, and trust him with the outcome?

Can you be thankful for where you and your child are?

Burdens can absolutely crush us. Some say that events are neutral; rather, it's how we handle them that can give us stress. We have to give those burdens up and pray for God's peace. One way to picture this is to imagine you are holding your child in your arms and then placing them at Jesus feet for him to watch over. Draw this image on this page.

What does it mean to me to become real?

Where can God take my spiritual life through this journey?

Song: *"All to Jesus, I Surrender"*
by Judson Van Deventer & Winfield Weeden

Journal or draw your thoughts from this lesson:

7

Learn How to Praise God . . .

. . . FOR WHOM HE IS AND WHAT HE'S DOING IN YOUR LIFE.

WHAT ARE YOU GAINING through this process? Are you gaining some character (Rom 5:3–5)? Are you gaining a higher level of trust in God? Are you surrendering your issues? Are you gaining a deeper "on your face" prayer life? Are you walking closer to God? How can you learn to be thankful in all circumstances (1 Thess 5:18)? Remember Job, who in the midst of losing almost everything, said in Job 1:21, "The Lord gave and the Lord has taken away; may the name of the Lord be praised." Sing praise, live praise by making it a daily sacrifice to God (Read Heb 13:15). Sacrifice is doing what we need to do when we don't want to do it or don't feel like doing it. But the sacrifice of praise is worth it when we find joy, peace, and an uplifted spirit when we express it. God wants us to praise him not just because he wants it, but because he knows we need it.

Praise is beyond the little sphere of our own individual life and surroundings; it is being amazed by a glorious God and praising God for who he is, what he has done, and what he is going to do. What if God is more able to use you and your child because of the rough season you're going through now? Second

Corinthians 1:3–4 says: "Praise be to the God and Father of our Lord Jesus Christ, the Father of compassion and the God of all comfort who comforts us in all our troubles, so that we can comfort those in any trouble with the comfort we ourselves have received from God." You will have more compassion for others who go through similar circumstances than you had before. God can use you better from the storms of your life than if you had stayed in the same place. There is a certain joy in being brought low, depending on God, and finding a greater closeness to him than ever before. Out of our pain comes pure joy in the Lord— refined and sincere—this joy brings forth sweet praise.

Find a joyful place to experience God's joy that is above your circumstances:

- *Make a Praise and Joy Basket:* Fill it with praise stories, stories of God's miracles and answers, jokes and funny stories, silly things that have happened to you, funny or cute pictures, photos, or items from special times.

- *Draw or Paint a Picture:* Create a picture of something meaningful to you, like Jesus holding you in his arms when you need to feel secure, peace, and loved.

- *Get Away:* Find something you enjoy doing to "get away" like spending time in nature (even your backyard), shopping, going to the salon, extra time in God's word, spending time with a friend, a soak in the tub, reading a good book, or petting the dog.

- *Enjoy Music:* Sing, listen to music, or play an instrument. Praise music can lift you up even when you don't feel like it.

- *Home Atmosphere:* Surround yourself with scriptures, music, and Christian speakers.

Remember the situation you are in is not your whole world, even though it may feel like it right now. Jesus is your whole world—focus on him by honoring, glorifying, and praising him. Seek God first and his righteousness. He is your whole purpose, your whole foundation, your whole *you*.

Questions to Help You Process:

What kind of character traits do I see, or hope to see, growing through my experience?

How can I help others who are hurting?

What could I put in a Praise and Joy basket?

What are some ways I can actively praise God? (for example, listening to the radio, CDs, singing, playing an instrument)

What kind of "joyful place" things am I going to put into action?

Where can God take my spiritual life through this journey?

***Songs**: "Praise You in this Storm" by Bernie Herns & Mark Hall and "Blessed Be the Name of the Lord" by Matt Redman*

Journal or draw your thoughts from this lesson:

8

Forgiveness . . .

. . . OF SELF, OF THE PERSON WHO CAUSED YOUR BROKEN
HEART, OF GOD, CULTURE AND OTHERS.

URN YOUR THOUGHTS AWAY from the whys and where-
fores, the blame game, resentment, revenge, and anger.
Learn to make a forgiving spirit your goal. When we
don't forgive we are dwelling on the past, not the present or the
future. When we can truly forgive we allow ourselves to be able
to heal and continue forward.

Forgiving Yourself

What is a perfect parent? Where do they get their affirmation:
from themselves, their children, spouse, family, workplace, society, or the government? Is there such a thing as a perfect parent?
We're all imperfect and vulnerable. We all make messes that we
can't take back. We daily pray for wisdom, insight and discern-
ment, but we are not all knowing and all seeing. We don't know
what is ahead. We don't know how our child will react to or perceive how each part of their life is handled. We are not perfect.

Only God is perfect and he is the one who can give true direction, wisdom, and love. Look at the past realistically. Grow from it and then press on toward the goal. You can't change the past no matter how hard you would like to. You can't change what has happened in the past, but you can change what happens now. You are more mature and have more experience with life now than you ever have had. Live in the now, striving to have no more regrets in your life. Be a better you.

Forgiving your Child

You can't change your child. They are unique and have a certain view of things. They are not you. Reasoning may not work. Yelling will not work. Manipulating does not work. If you can forgive them and move on, though, your heart will be clear and you will gain the ability to deal with them without a perpetual "chip on your shoulder." Let go of the idea that your child should get what they deserve from their choices. We aren't called to judge. We are called to love unconditionally. How many people come to Christ because they are yelled at, lectured at, or coerced? Most people come because of unconditional love—you know, that's how God loves us.

Forgiving God

In the psalms, David spends a lot of time wondering where God is and what he's doing. But he always holds on to a thread of hope that God will work out his situation and praises God in the end. Let God be God. Trust his plan. It's bigger than you are and different than you may realize. Isaiah 55:8 says it well: "For my thoughts are not your thoughts, neither are your ways my ways, declares the Lord."

Forgiving your Culture

Certainly, the condition of our culture is a mess. Our kids get caught up in lots of junk from mainstream culture: fads like piercings and tattoos, issues that are hyped up in the media, drugs and alcohol, materialism, sex, and all the different issues that these activities entail. Unfortunately, we can't do much to change the entire world (except pray, help others, and try to be a godly example). We can't hide our child away from worldliness forever. But living with aggravation and frustration about the world doesn't help us either—it just takes away our peace.

Forgiving Others

We could blame our spouse, our busybody neighbor, our bad-example relatives, our child's crazy friends, their spouse, their new religion or community, but blaming doesn't help. Instead, it keeps us living in frustration. It can become a treadmill that winds around and around and gets us nowhere.

On a vacation in Indiana one year, my husband David, our two girls, and I ate at a series of restaurants. Meal after meal one or the other of our daughters knocked over a glass of water. It happened at several meals. One night at the dinner table, I jokingly spoke up before the meal and asked the girls to please be careful and not spill any more glasses of water. Before five minutes passed, I reached for an item and knocked my glass of water pell-mell all over the table. Can you imagine the blush I had on my face as I had done what I cautioned the girls not to do? We are all sinners. Before we point our finger at someone else's sin, before we think we are better, before we say, "You blew it," we need to take a look at ourselves and realize where we would be if Jesus hadn't forgiven us. Try to not allow pride and an unforgiving attitude take charge of you and what you say. Mercy and unconditional love is what others need from us, because that's what we get from God. If we can live without blame and have a forgiving heart, we will not only greatly help ourselves, but those around us will see an example of why Christ came to be a sacrifice for our sins.

Questions to Help You Process:

Whom do I have the hardest time forgiving and why?

What do I need to do about my unforgiving spirit?

How can I live out forgiveness to those who have deeply hurt me?

Do I carry a perpetual "chip on my shoulder?"

Do I use judging terms or loving terms when I talk about others?

How can I show mercy and unconditional love to someone and still
hold on to my values?

Where can God take my spiritual life through this journey?

Song*: "Forgiveness" by Matthew West*

Journal or draw your thoughts from this lesson:

9

Can I Let Jesus Shine?

WHEN MY HUSBAND DAVID and I were first married, our youth group sent us to Hawaii for our honeymoon. When we got back, my new father-in-law had painted our little home. It was painted a very distinct, bright pink color. I was shocked. I had plans to paint our house with the then-popular earth tones of the 1970s—but it was bright pink with white trim. David found out that his dad had found the paint on sale and bought it. He wanted to surprise us with a fresh coat of paint, so he painted it while we were gone. What could I say? We lived with the bright pink house for a year and a half. Our teens claimed that it "glowed in the dark" and that no one could possibly miss it when we had a youth activity there. We are to be a bright and guiding light for Christ, especially to our children. Nothing is as appealing to others as the true joy a real Christian shines out of their life—even if it's "pink." That only happens when you find a deep awareness of Christ walking with you through each day. Spend time surrounded by Bible scriptures, music, and hearing God's word preached and talked about so that your life will be encompassed by a glow of Jesus that others will see and hopefully want for themselves. Seek his face daily. Hold on to Jesus. Be tenacious in holding firm to him. Think of him as your firm foundation, because he is. Everything else is "sinking sand."

Knowledge in the scriptures helps us shine when we aren't looking at God's word but still need its strength and encouragement. At a recent women's retreat one of the speakers talked about how in the past, she had such a hard time memorizing the scriptures and she struggled to learn them. Then she had a breakthrough that really helped her—she used drawings to represent the words and phrases. It helped her to learn God's word in a more visual way.

Try not to be fake about shining either. We can get used to acting and saying things in church language. Remember that some of the people you're communicating with may not have ever been to church and will get lost trying to figure out what you are trying to say. My best times of talking to others about what Christ means to me is when I've been through a rotten time in my life and can say how deeply my relationship to Christ has become through it and why. People would rather hear about your personal walk with Christ than the entire "lingo" you learned to say in church. People want to see how you deal with life and how you can stand up under all the junk that gets thrown at you. Yes, yours may be a time of sincere stress and pressure, but that's how diamonds are formed. After a diamond is made by pressure then it is cut to bring out of high quality of its shine. Let God cut away what brings out the shine in you.

Before Stephen was martyred in Acts 7, he witnessed to the Sanhedrin and was full of the Holy Spirit. Surely the people saw God's glory in him. But still they stoned him. Why? They had hardened their hearts. Stephen was so full of God's spirit that his concern wasn't his life or the "how dare they stone me" thoughts, but prayer for those who were stoning him and their welfare. He asked for God to forgive them. I pray that we can be so in tune with Christ that no matter what others say or do to us, we are filled with love for them and for God.

Shining for the Lord is to know and experience his glory. No matter how God's glory is received, it is there. Our ability to shine is between God and us. What others see is just our relationship with God spilling out. This is not an act or a test of how well trained we are to witness; rather, it is between God and us, with others seeing the results.

Questions to Help You Process:

How can God turn around my situation for his glory?

How can I shine when my heart is broken?

Is my God the God I love and enjoy beyond my earthly pain?

Do I let my earthly pain blot out my God?

Can I shine and be real—not fake?

How can I be more real in how I act and what I say?

What does God need to cut or trim away from me to make the shine come out better?

Does it matter if the person we're talking with believes our message? Why or why not?

Where can God take my spiritual life through this journey?

Song: "Shine, Jesus, Shine" by Cliff Richard

Journal or draw your thoughts from this lesson:

Three Great Areas:
Faith, Hope, and Love

Faith.

HOLD ON TO YOUR faith. "Jesus Christ is the same yester-day, today, and forever" (Heb 13:8). He is our anchor, our rock, and our fortress—he is consistent. It's wonderful to have a God who doesn't change and who is a rock that doesn't move. Our relationships change, our emotions change, society changes, the securities of this world change, but God is unchanging. Everyone has something or someone they believe in. Why not have faith in someone who has stood the test of time, who has been there and knows what is going on in your life and in your mind, who loves you and who died for you?

Hope.

Without hope our dreams die. Hope is what we look forward to and what keeps us going. You may have to adjust or put on hold the dreams, plans, and goals you wished for your child, but don't allow circumstances try to rob you of your hope. Real hope remains solid. First Corinthians 13:13 says, "these three remain: Faith, Hope, and Love."

Love.

When my children have needed more attention, I've tried to put out even more effort to show them my love and God's love. Scriptures around the home are silent reminders to them how perfectly God loves us. Isaiah 54:10 says: "Though the mountains be shaken and the hills be removed, yet my unfailing love for you will not be shaken nor my covenant of peace be removed says the Lord, who has compassion on you." God is our example of steadfast love. Loving our children as Christ loves them is something we can always do. Everyone needs love. Love is the best motivator. Hebrews 10:24 says, "let us consider how we may spur one another on toward love and good deeds."

A friend of mine went through a difficult period several years ago. She decided to stand with one of her children through a messy divorce. Her other children didn't agree with her and turned their backs on her and their sibling. She found herself in a very hard spot. Supporting one child meant not supporting the feelings of her other children. She said:

> "Having three of my children stop speaking to me or having any kind of fellowship with me was almost too hard to bear. I could not have found the strength to overcome my feeling of my broken heart without the Lord. Only God could take that kind of pain away. I struggled every moment to try to understand why this was happening. Being faithful was something I had to do to show my children that Christ's love is unconditional. You have to show your love no matter what people say or how they treat you. By going through this time with my children I had to learn that my desire for approval from my children could only be met by receiving God's acceptance and approval. Not by my children's.
>
> I learned and grew so much during the four years that I was walking through this storm. The most important

thing I did learn is that you have to wait on God, have grace, mercy, and love for people, and never compromise your convictions to keep you from being rejected. I stood by my conviction and that was standing by the truth. My daughter and I were brought through this storm by God's grace and mercy. My children and I are now on the road of healing and working on a functional relationship with one another. My daughter and I have a lot to be thankful for but most of all, we give all the glory to God."

Faith, hope, and love in Jesus are what we can hold on to and what brings us through the storms of our lives—and we do and will have storms!

Questions to Help You Process:

Is my faith where I would like it to be?

What would my faith be like if it was what I desired it to be?

What do I hope for?

Have I allowed hope to be taken away from me?

How can I show love to my family?

What ways do my family need to be loved?

Is it possible that my child's behavior is a hidden deep desire for my love and approval in their life?

How do I want God to help me to be a more loving person?

What am I willing to do to stand firm in what I know to be true?

Where can God take my spiritual life through this journey?

Song*: "Love Divine, All Loves Excelling"*
by Charles Wesley & John Zundel

Journal or draw your thoughts from this lesson:

II

Pray with All You've Got

WE ARE TOLD, IN 1 Thess 5:17, to pray continuously and without ceasing. Ephesians 6:12 states that our battle is not against flesh and blood but against "principalities and powers." Matthew 5:23–24 tells us to clear the air: leave your gift at altar and go make other relationships as right as you can so you will be able to pray. James 1:6 says, believe in what you are praying for and believe in the God you are praying to. Where we can't pray deep enough or without the fullness of his knowledge, he intercedes for us (Rom 8:26). Pray for God's perfect will to be done (Luke 22:42). When Jesus asked for God's will and not his own, he had to let go of his own human desires and submit to what divinely needed to be done. Can you let go of your will and let God have his? In other words, in prayer you don't always get your way. So don't be disappointed in God when he answers things differently than the way you think you want it answered. Don't tell others that God didn't answer your prayer because things happen differently than you want them to. His answers don't have to fit in our own particular boxes. He answers in his own time, will, and way.

Read about fasting in Isaiah 58. In Mark, Jesus says that some things can only be done through prayer and fasting. Do you have a problem with fasting that makes you dizzy or feel sick? In the past, it has helped me to fast an item—like meat or dessert—for a week or so while still eating regular meals. Maybe it means giving up a snack time or drinking only water instead of coffee or tea. Maybe it means giving up an activity, like watching TV. Fasting *is* an important part of praying for the super serious requests and needs in your life. It deepens our prayers and helps us to be submissive to God's perfect will. Carefully consider this area of prayer in your life. Be aware of your dietary and physical needs and contact your doctor if you have concerns. You can also look at different ideas for fasting.

Sometimes I have wondered if my prayers are good enough. Am I missing a "secret code" or "key?" I've heard others say that God answered their prayers because they did this or that. God just wants to hear your heart. There isn't a "secret code" and when you are submissive to him there is no "hidden key." We just need faith the size of a mustard seed. The size of our faith doesn't have to do with his strength.

One day, I was on my face, on the floor praying in despair. I had fasted and prayed about something that God didn't take away. I knew I was praying in his will. Why couldn't he answer it now? When I got up from my prayer time I didn't feel any better. But as the day went on I felt increasing peace. I felt God was telling me it was all in his hands and for me to be a shining light for him even though the issue wouldn't go away. I also felt a deep sense of his love and presence overwhelming me. God is always in the process of answering prayers. He just wants us to trust, be obedient to him, and let others see Jesus' love in us.

Prayer can be done in many ways: out loud or in our heads, singing a song, signing, writing or drawing, expressing yourself in choreography, quoting scriptures. I had the most wonderful experience praying in song one day. I used the tune of a hymn and put in my prayers for those things that were heavy on my heart. It wasn't necessary for it to rhyme, but it just came out in such a sweet and meaningful way that I felt really close to God's throne.

Questions to Help You Process:

How do I know when to stop and leave my requests in God's hands?
What about the parable of the persistent widow in Luke 18:1–8?

When does persistence become too consuming?

What does fasting mean to me?

How can I put fasting into action for my family?

What kind of answers do I want from God?

What does praying in God's will mean?

If I feel that I am praying in God's will, can I let him have his way about it?

Draw your deepest prayer:

Where can God take my spiritual life through this journey?

Song: "Sweet Hour of Prayer"
by William Walford & William Bradbury

Journal or draw your thoughts from this lesson:

12

To Encourage You

YOU ARE NOT ALONE. There are others going through heartbreak with their children. There has already been a lot of healing in my relationship with my older daughter and I'm so very thankful for it. Our children are very precious to us—more than they realize. I pray for you as you go through your journey. I know it is difficult and can easily throw a person off track. But I also know that God wants to make you a better person through it. He wants to draw you closer and help you realize how much he loves you in this storm. God answers everyone's prayers differently: some take time, some may have twists in the road, and some may come quickly. To encourage you, please read this true story of a daughter who came back to the Lord in a strong and powerful way.

The Story of a Real Prodigal Daughter:

"Don't ever give up. Don't ever give up praying for your children and don't ever lose hope that God is working in their lives, even when you can't see it. If you've raised your child in a Christian home, with Christian values, and have exposed them to the ways of the Lord, then don't ever doubt that this upbringing was lost on them or that all they have been taught has fallen on deaf ears.

I am the adult child of parents that faithfully prayed over me. One of my regrets is that neither of them got to see the results of their prayers as I've come back into a right relationship with God. Truly, he has been faithful in restoring the years the locusts have eaten during the time I walked away from him.

I was raised in the "ideal" Christian home with loving parents and grandparents that loved and served the Lord wholeheartedly. It was their longing and desire that their children and their children's children would all grow to do the same love the Lord our God with all of our hearts, souls, and minds and serve him faithfully all the days of our lives.

As a child I loved going to church, Sunday School, Children's Church, Vacation Bible School, and "Missionettes"—my mother and grandmother were right there leading it all. My father was right there, as well, leading Sunday School classes, Royal Rangers, and taking on leadership roles by serving on various boards. My mom played the piano and organ for the church and my dad ran special events. They ran the bus ministry together, picking up kids all over the town so they could come to church on Sundays and Wednesday nights. Often, we would travel to other churches in our district for speaking engagements for my father. My grandparents even cleaned the church, so my brother and I were often at the church even when the doors weren't "open."

As I got older, opportunities to get involved in leadership roles myself were offered and you would often find me leading Bible studies and serving on the Youth Council, mentoring younger kids.

To say that I was "born and raised" in the church is an understatement. I don't even think that there were pastor's kids that spent more time in church and doing church activities as my brother and I. And still, I rebelled.

I started to rebel during my teen years and for some time I played the role of "good Christian daughter," as well as being the kind of person the world would consider cool.

As well intentioned as my parents were, I believe the mistake they made raising us was being overly—and I do mean overly—protective and strict. Please don't get me wrong. Children must have boundaries. They must be taught right from wrong. However, there must also be a balance in raising our children that shows them that not only do we believe in them to make the right decision and give them the opportunity to do so, we need to show them that we trust God to watch over them, protect them and to lead them and guide them to what is right according to his will.

For me, the rebellion started very simply with that first lie—a lie that I told my parents in order to go to a movie at the age of thirteen or fourteen (we were not allowed to go to the movies). I remember that the movie was *Rocky* with Sylvester Stallone. I can even remember the specific movie theater. All of my friends were going to movies, so what was the big deal? The big deal is that this lie led to more lies, which opened the door for the enemy to begin his work in my life.

I could probably write my own book about all that I went through during my time of not walking with the Lord—teenage pregnancy, drugs, illegal activity, etc.—but that's not the point of my contribution to the book you are reading. My point is to tell you there is hope—that's the happy ending. I believe that no one is ever beyond redemption, surely not if the Lord can take the mess of a life I was living and turn it completely around.

Through the faithful prayers of many and by the grace of God, I never had my children taken away. I overcame drug addictions that were so intense that I was beyond addicted; I was dependent on them to function.

Most people I know today would never guess by looking at me, or knowing me, that I ever led a life that consisted of such things. I've been married to a wonderful man for close to twenty years and have three amazing adult children. My husband and I have a successful business and are involved in our community and serve on various boards.

We are honored and privileged to lead a Sunday School class at our church and serve on our Missions

Board together. For the past five years, God has allowed me to lead a life group every week with some of the most amazing ladies I've ever known. This last year we had the awesome opportunity to go to Argentina on our first, of what we hope to be many, missions trip together and the Lord has blessed me with the opportunity to go to Haiti twice last year and begin a nonprofit that serves the educational and spiritual needs of children in a remote village.

So my message is simple: Don't give up. Don't ever give up praying and don't ever give up hope because the Lord *will* restore the years the locusts have eaten, just as he has promised. Remember, too, that as much as you love your child, God loves them more. Cling to that truth."

No one knows, as well as you, what you need to heal your relationship with your child. You can get advice, find resources, ask for prayer, and get counseling but you need to find the right fit and find the correct direction God would have you go in. This is because you have to live with your decisions, reactions, and goals like no one else does. With love, prayer, and God's word you can head towards healing your heart and your relationship with your child. May God bless you in your journey and "don't ever give up hope."

Questions to Help You Process:

How can I encourage myself?

How can I encourage others?

What does it mean to me to "never give up?"

What do I gain if I give up?

What does the story of the "prodigal daughter" say that encourages you?

Do I have ideas on what to do from here and what direction God would like me to go in?

Where can God take my spiritual life through this journey?

Song: "Great is Thy Faithfulness"
by Thomas Chisholm & William Runyan

Journal or draw your thoughts from this lesson:

Other Helpful Scripture References

(NIV Version)

"God is our refuge and strength, an ever-present help in trouble. Therefore we will not fear, though the earth give way and the mountains fall into the heart of the sea, though its waters roar and foam and the mountains quake with their surging."

PSALM 46:1–3

"Jesus answered, "What is impossible with men is possible with God."

LUKE 18:27

"You are my hiding place; you will protect me from trouble and surround me with songs of deliverance."

PSALM 32:7

"Rejoice in the Lord always, I will say it again: Rejoice! Let you gentleness be evident to all. The Lord is near. Do not be anxious about anything, but in everything by prayer and petition, with thanksgiving, present your requests to God and the peace of God, which transcends all understanding, will guard your hears and your minds in Christ

Jesus."

PHILIPPIANS 4:4-7

"'Because he loves me,' says the Lord, 'I will protect him, for he ac-
knowledges my name. He will call upon me and I will answer him;
I will be with him in trouble, I will deliver him and honor him. With
long life will I satisfy him and show him my salvation.'"

PSALM 91:14-16

"Finally, brothers, whatever is true, whatever is noble, whatever is
right, whatever is pure, whatever is lovely, whatever is admirable-if
anything is excellent or praiseworthy-think about such things."

PHILIPPIANS 4:8

"Jesus said . . . 'Don't be afraid; just believe.'"

MARK 5:36

"Be joyful always; pray continually; give thanks in all circumstances,
for this is God's will for you in Christ Jesus. Do not put out the Spirit's
fire; do not treat prophecies with contempt. Test everything. Hold on
to the good. Avoid every kind of evil. May God himself, the God of
peace, sanctify you through and through. May your whole spirit, soul
and body be kept blameless at the coming of our Lord Jesus Christ.
The one who calls you is faithful and he will do it."

1 THESSALONIANS 5:16-24

"Do you not know? Have you not heard? The Lord is the everlasting
God, the Creator of the ends of the earth. He will not grow tired or
weary, and his understanding no one can fathom. He gives strength
to the weary and increases the power of the weak. Even youths grow
tired and weary, and young men stumble and fall; but those who hope

in the Lord will renew their strength. They will soar on wings like eagles; they will run and not grow weary, they will walk and not be faint."

ISAIAH 40:28–31

"Moses answered the people, 'Do not be afraid. Stand firm and you will see the deliverance the Lord will bring you today. The Lord will fight for you; you need only to be still."

EXODUS 14:13–14

"This is what the Lord says to you: 'Do not be afraid or discouraged because of this vast army. For the battle is not yours, but God's."

2 CHRONICLES 20:15

"So do not fear, for I am with you; do not be dismayed, for I am your God. I will strengthen you and help you; I will uphold you with my righteous right hand."

ISAIAH 41:10

"'If you can?' said Jesus. 'Everything is possible for him who believes.' Immediately the boy's father exclaimed, 'I do believe; help me overcome my unbelief!'"

MARK 9:23-24

"But he said to me, 'My grace is sufficient for you, for my power is made perfect in weakness.' Therefore I will boast all the more gladly about my weaknesses, so that Christ's power may rest on me. That is why, for Christ's sake, I delight in weaknesses, in insults, in hardships, in persecutions, in difficulties. For when I am weak, then I am strong."

2 CORINTHIANS 12 9–10

"... 'Fear not, for I have redeemed you; I have summoned you by name you are mine. When you pass through the waters, I will be with you; and when you pass through the rivers, they will not sweep over you. When you walk through the fire, you will not be burned; the flames will not set you ablaze.'"

ISAIAH 43:1–2

"'Though the mountains be shaken and the hills be removed, yet my unfailing love for you will not be shaken nor my covenant of peace be removed,' says the Lord, who has compassion on you."

ISAIAH 54:10

Add scriptures that are helpful to you:

Daily Devotional Sample

Bible Study

Gratitude: I am thankful for . . . (list at least five things)

Bible Reading

Old Testament Scriptures:

My Thoughts:

New Testament Scriptures:

My Thoughts:

Prayer

What I'm Dealing With:

Anger/Resentments

Forgiving

Issues

Feelings

Surrendering

Fears

Other

Characteristics I would like to see grow in my life:

Those on My Heart:

Family:

Church:

Work:

Friends:

Others:

Those I'm burdened for:

Missionaries:

Country:

World:

More:

Worship and Praise

Play favorite CDs, radio programs, etc.

Sing favorite hymns, choruses, etc.

Quote favorite scriptures